ABUNDANT TRUTH INTERN

MW00851614

Kingdom Stewards Series

THE PROPHETIC MINISTRY

"Exploring the Prophetic Office and Gift"

By: Roderick L. Evans

Abundant Truth PUBLISHING
abundantpublishing.net
P.O. Box 126, Camden, NC 27921

Published by Abundant Truth Publishing
P.O. Box 126
Camden, NC 27921
Phone: 1-877-938-3930* Fax: 1-877-938-3930
Web: www.abundantpublishing.net
Email: abundantpublishing@gmail.com

Printed U.S.A.

Front & Back Cover Designs by Abundant Truth Publishing
All rights reserved.

Abundant Truth Publishing is a ministry of **Abundant Truth International Ministries.** The primary mission of ATI Ministries is to equip the Body of Christ with tools necessary to defend and contend for the truth of the Christian faith. Jesus Christ came to bear witness of the truth and ATI Ministries is a modern-day extension of His commission (John 18:37).

Kingdom Stewards – The Prophetic Ministry
©2005 Abundant Truth Publishing
All Rights Reserved

ISBN: 978-1-60141-048-1

Table of Contents

Preface
Introduction

Chapter 1 – What is a Prophet?   **1**

Prophets in the Old Testament   *2*
Prophets in the New Testament   *5*

Chapter 2 – The Office of the Prophet   **13**

Prophets as Messengers   *13*
Prophets as Interpreters   *16*
Nine Functions of the Prophet   *17*
Focus of Prophets21

Chapter 3 – What is Prophecy?   **23**

The Gift of Prophecy   *23*
The Prophetic Anointing   *25*
The Prophetic Office   *26*
The Spirit of Prophecy   *26*

Chapter 4 – The Prophetic Vehicle   **29**

Voice of the Lord   *30*
Dreams and Visions   *31*
Prophetic Perception   *32*
Prophetic Events   *33*
Prayer   *35*
Angels   *36*
The Scriptures   *37*

Chapter 5 – The Prophetic Perspective   **39**

Guidelines for Receiving Prophecy   *40*
Guidelines for Judging Prophecy   *43*
Guidelines for Applying Prophecy   *47*

Preface

Peter told the believers that they were **stewards** of the manifold grace of God. This means that every follower of Christ has the responsibility to grow and develop in their God-given gifts. In addition, they are to be faithful in ministering to others. The Kingdom Steward Series was created to help believers understand their gifts and ministries. It is designed to bring clarity to the purpose and functions of spiritual gifts and ministries. It is our prayer that believers will grow in the recognition, acceptance, and operation of the gifts of God.

In this publication:

This publication presents a solid introduction to the prophetic ministry. It will bring clarity and understanding to the prophetic office, the prophetic anointing, and the gift of prophecy. This information will help individuals to recognize the operations of this anointing in their lives and in the lives of others. It is our hope that believers will develop a greater respect and appreciation for the prophetic office and gift.

1
What is a Prophet?

The prophets are here! God always spoke to His people through the ministry of the prophets. After the Church was established, prophets continued to minister. The ministry of prophets did not cease after the deaths of the first century apostles and prophets. Some scholars have promoted the idea that since we have scripture, there is no need for prophetic ministry. Others believe that since the Holy Spirit is in all believers, prophetic ministry is useless.

However, we should know that these doctrines are incorrect. Prophets and prophetic ministry are essential to God's purpose for the Church. God established this ministry in the Church second only to apostolic ministry.

The word prophet originates from the Greek word, *prophetes,* which means an inspired speaker or a foreteller. Prophets will only speak for God, not for a particular Church or organization. Prophets are chosen to communicate the heart and mind of God. They are specialists in "the word of the Lord." Prophets' ministries will vary in demonstration and expression.

> *Surely, the Lord God will do nothing, but he revealeth his secret unto his servants the prophets. (Amos 3:7)*

From the above verse and numerous examples in scripture, we know that prophets have a unique place in the kingdom of God.

Prophets in the Old Testament

Before and after the establishment of the Mosaic Law and Old Covenant, prophets were used by God. The scriptures tell us of the prophetic ministry of Enoch. Abel, Adam's son, is listed among those who are considered prophets.

> *That the blood of all the **prophets**, which was shed from the foundation of the world, may be required of this generation; From the blood of **Abel** unto the blood of Zacharias, which perished between the altar and the temple: verily I say unto you, It shall be required of this generation.(Luke11:50-51, Emphasis Mine)*

> *And **Enoch** also, the seventh from Adam, **prophesied** of these, saying, Behold, the Lord cometh with ten thousands of his saints. (Jude 1:14 Emphasis Mine)*

Aside from these, there are others, before the Law, who were prophets. One well-known prophet is Abraham. While rebuking Abimelech, God calls him a prophet.

> *Now therefore restore the man his wife; for he is a prophet, and he shall pray for thee, and thou shalt live: and if thou restore her not, know thou that thou shalt surely die, thou, and all that are thine.(Genesis 20:7)*

Abraham's prophetic status was evident because of how the Lord used him. Abraham was used to represent the voice of the Lord in the earth. In addition, God revealed to him future events in his life and others (Sodom/Gomorrah and his descendants), as well as His eternal purpose. Even Christ said that Abraham saw His day before He came.

> *Your father Abraham rejoiced to see my day: and he saw it, and was glad. (John 8:56)*

Aside from Abraham, we see the greatest expression of the prophetic ministry after the institution of the Law. God used Moses, a prophet, to reveal His will for man's service to Him. After these things, God sent the prophets to Israel to cause them to return to Him and walk in His ways.

> *Since the day that your fathers came forth out of the land of Egypt unto this day I have even sent unto you all my servants the prophets, daily rising up early and sending them. (Jeremiah 7:25)*

In the Old Testament, the prophets came to perform certain tasks. God used the prophets to represent His voice to Israel and the surrounding nations. In the writings of Jeremiah, Ezekiel, and others, we see prophetic revelation concerning the nations. Also, God used the prophets to reveal God's plans for Israel and Judah even after He disciplined them.

> *I have also spoken by the prophets, and I have multiplied visions, and used similitudes, by the ministry of the prophets. (Hosea 12:10)*

The prophets had the task of challenging the sins of the people, calling them back into fellowship with God. The prophets were also excellent interpreters of the Law through divine inspiration. Through their ministries, they would correct erroneous doctrines surrounding the Law.

> *And thou shalt say unto them, Thus saith the Lord; If ye will not hearken to me, to walk in my law, which I have set before you, to hearken to the words of my servants the prophets, whom I sent unto you, both rising up early, and sending them, but ye have not hearkened. (Jeremiah 26:4-5)*

The prophets of the Old Testament cried out against false prophets; revealing wolves in sheep's clothing.

> *Then the Lord said unto me, The prophets prophesy lies in my name: I sent them not, neither have I commanded them, neither spake unto them: they prophesy unto you a false vision and divination, and a thing of nought, and the deceit of their heart. (Jeremiah 14:14)*

> *Son of man, prophesy against the prophets of Israel that prophesy, and say thou unto them that prophesy out of their own hearts, Hear ye the word of the Lord; Thus saith the Lord God; Woe unto the foolish prophets, that follow their own spirit, and have seen nothing! O Israel, thy prophets are like the foxes in the deserts. Ye have not gone up into the gaps, neither made up the hedge for the house of Israel to stand in the battle in the day of the Lord. They have seen vanity and lying divination, saying, The Lord saith: and the Lord hath not sent them: and they have made others to hope that they would confirm the word. (Ezekiel 13:2-6)*

In addition to the above tasks, the prophets revealed God's plan for individuals as well as God's eternal purpose.

Consider Jeremiah's words. He revealed God's purpose of redemption and salvation for Israel as a nation.

The prophets of old were not only men of rebuke and correction, but also men of vision and insight into God's good will for His people. Much of the recorded prophetic ministry came at a time when Israel and Judah were rebellious. However, the scriptures reveal that God had more to say to them than just repent. He wanted them to know His eternal plan and purpose for them as a nation.

> *Behold, the days come, saith the Lord, that I will make a new covenant with the house of Israel, and with the house of Judah. (Jeremiah 31:31)*

Therefore, we see that prophets have been around from the beginning. They have always been a part of God's working in the earth. With the establishment of the New Covenant and the Church, this did not change.

Prophets in the New Testament

After the establishment of the Church, God still used prophets. New Testament prophets fulfill the same functions as their Old Testament counterparts. They represent the voice of the Lord to the Church and world (however, this is done alongside other believers and ministers). They are to be preachers of the Gospel of Jesus Christ. They challenge believers in their walks with the Lord. They call the Church to change and repentance and reveal future events. In addition to the above functions, the New Testament prophet serves as a foundational ministry to the Church.

On the day of Pentecost, God established His will for man's worship. He no longer wanted to be "confined" to a building (represented by God's command to worship at the Temple), but dwell in the hearts of man. His will was for the believer to be His temple. As He abides in each individual, they corporately become the temple of God. Peter called the believers "stones" who are built together to form a spiritual house or temple where God could dwell.

> *Ye also, as lively stones, are built up a spiritual house, an holy priesthood, to offer up spiritual sacrifices, acceptable to God by Jesus Christ. (I Peter 2:5)*

> *What? Know ye not that your body is the temple of the Holy Ghost which is in you, which ye have of God, and ye are not your own? (I Corinthians 6:19)*

With the New Covenant, the temple of God is now the hearts and minds of people. Their actual bodies become the habitation of God. Therefore, if the Church consists of people joined together by the presence of the Holy Spirit, then the foundation for the Church would consist of people also.

As Paul wrote to the believers, he revealed to them a very important truth. He told them that they (the Church) were built upon the foundation of the apostles and **prophets** with Christ being the head stone.

> *Now therefore ye are no more strangers and foreigners, but fellowcitizens with the saints, and of the household of God; And are built upon the foundation of the apostles and prophets, Jesus Christ himself being the chief corner stone; In whom all the building fitly framed together groweth unto an holy temple in the Lord: In whom ye also*

are builded together for an habitation of God through the Spirit. (Ephesians 2:19-22).

In the above scripture, we discover certain truths. Paul was writing to a primarily Gentile audience. However, we must understand that the foundation that they stood upon was the same as the Jewish believers. Jewish and Gentile believers, alike, operated in the foundation established by the New Testament apostles and **prophets**.

The Church, like the New Covenant, was founded upon people, namely, the apostles and **prophets**. From this, we understand that since we will reign with Christ, God allowed man to have an active role in the establishment of the Church.

The apostles and **prophets** bear the responsibility for the Church, especially in doctrinal purity and spiritual direction. As Christ formed the foundation for the New Covenant, the apostles and **prophets** formed the foundation for the Church. Their ministries are foundational and continue to be major influences upon the Body of Christ.

The ministries of the apostles and **prophets** were needed to establish the Church, and their ministries are needed presently for the furtherance of the Church. Christ's ministry toward us is everlasting.

> *But this man, because he continueth ever, hath an unchangeable priesthood. Wherefore he is able also to save them to the uttermost that come unto God by him, seeing he ever liveth to make intercession for them. (Hebrews 7:24-25)*

The Book of Acts reveals to us the presence of prophets in the New Testament Church. Consider the following:

7

> *And in these days came prophets from Jerusalem*
> *unto Antioch. And there stood up one of them*
> *named Agabus, and signified by the spirit that there*
> *should be great dearth throughout all the world:*
> *which came to pass in the days of Claudius Caesar.*
> *(Acts 11:27-28)*

The early Church benefited from the ministry of the prophets. We discover that the prophets traveled together.

A prophet of note among them was named **Agabus**. Through his ministry, the saints were prepared for a drought that came. They responded in sending help to the brethren that would be affected. Agabus also prepared Paul for the trials that awaited him in Jerusalem through prophetic insight.

> *And as we tarried there many days, there came*
> *down from Judaea a certain prophet, named*
> *Agabus. And when he was come unto us, he took*
> *Paul's girdle, and bound his own hands and feet,*
> *and said, Thus saith the Holy Ghost, So shall the*
> *Jews at Jerusalem bind the man that owneth this*
> *girdle, and shall deliver him into the hands of the*
> *Gentiles.(Acts 21:10-11)*

Aside from the foretelling of future events, we also discover that the New Testament prophet would strengthen and encourage the brethren through his ministry.

> *And Judas and Silas, being prophets also*
> *themselves, exhorted the brethren with many words,*
> *and confirmed them. (Acts 15:32)*

Judas and Silas were recognized prophets in the early Church. They accompanied Paul and Barnabas back to Antioch with the elders' response to the requirements of Gentile believers. The above verse demonstrates to us that the prophet's ministry came to push the believers forward and establish them in the things of the Lord. In addition, we discover that when Silas joined Paul on his missionary journey that great ministry followed.

Not only did the New Testament prophets reveal future events and encourage the brethren, but also they helped to launch ministries through prophetic insight.

> *Now there were in the church that was at Antioch certain prophets and teachers; as Barnabas, and Simeon that was called Niger, and Lucius of Cyrene, and Manaen, which had been brought up with Herod the tetrarch, and Saul. As they ministered to the Lord, and fasted, the Holy Ghost said, Separate me Barnabas and Saul for the work whereunto I have called them. (Acts 13:1-2)*

In the Antioch church, it is apparent that prophets and teachers exercised the oversight. We find that as they ministered unto the Lord, the Lord spoke (it is likely through one of the prophets) to release Saul and Barnabas into the apostolic ministry. Saul (Paul) and Barnabas were recognized among the prophets and teachers.

However, through prophetic ministry, they were called forward to operate in another ministry. The New Testament prophet will do this occasionally. Along with the ministry of the prophets, the Book of Acts introduces us to individuals who had prophetic ministries and the gift of prophecy.

After Saul's (Paul's) conversion, the Lord spoke to a certain disciple named Ananias in a vision.

And there was a certain disciple at Damascus, named Ananias; and to him said the Lord in a vision, Ananias. And he said, Behold, I am here, Lord. And the Lord said unto him, Arise, and go into the street which is called Straight, and inquire in the house of Judas for one called Saul, of Tarsus: for, behold, he prayeth, And hath seen in a vision a man named Ananias coming in, and putting his hand on him, that he might receive his sight. Then Ananias answered, Lord, I have heard by many of this man, how much evil he hath done to thy saints at Jerusalem: And here he hath authority from the chief priests to bind all that call on thy name. But the Lord said unto him, Go thy way: for he is a chosen vessel unto me, to bear my name before the Gentiles, and kings, and the children of Israel: For I will shew him how great things he must suffer for my name's sake.(Acts 9:10-16)

The scriptures do not identify Ananias as a prophet, but a disciple. However, the depth of revelation and power that he operated in shows us that he walked in a prophetic anointing. God spoke to him personally. God's interaction with him is similar to how the Lord would speak to prophets.

When we consider other notable figures such as Peter (an apostle) and Philip (an evangelist and one of the seven), it is evident that these men possessed a prophetic anointing, though they were not prophets.

The scriptures not only reveal to us individuals who were prophets and had a prophetic anointing, but also those who had the gift of prophecy. Philip, the evangelist, had four daughters that had the gift of prophecy. Some scholars want to identify them as prophetesses. However, the most popular translations of this passage in Acts only refer to them as having the gift of prophecy. They did not occupy the prophetic office.

> *And the next day we that were of Paul's company departed, and came unto Caesarea: and we entered into the house of Philip the evangelist, which was one of the seven; and abode with him. And the same man had four daughters, virgins, which did prophesy. (Acts 21:8-9 KJV)*

> *And he had four maiden daughters who had the gift of prophecy. (Acts 21:9 Amplified)*

> *He had four unmarried daughters who prophesied (Acts 21:9 NIV)*

From the above scriptures and references, we discover that the New Testament Church had prophets, individuals who possessed a prophetic anointing, and those who had the gift of prophecy. These gifts were needed then and they are needed now.

There are theologians who twist the scriptures. In doing so, they assert that because we have the canon of scripture that prophets, prophetic ministry, and the gift of prophecy are no longer needed. The scriptures declare that Jesus Christ is the same yesterday, today, and forever (Hebrews 13:8). He ministered to the early Church through the prophets. He will not change until the end of all things.

If He used prophets and prophetic ministry in those times, He will continue to do so. Christ's ministry to the Church will not end until the Judgment; therefore, the ministries of the prophets will not end until that Day. God is still using prophets today. In addition, God is raising up individuals who walk under and in an prophetic anointing that His glory may be seen in all.

2

The Office of the Prophet

We have discussed what a prophet is. Though not all prophets are the same, there are certain characteristics that they possess. All prophets exhibit characteristics of messengers and interpreters.

Prophets as Messengers

God calls prophets for one purpose. They are to be His messengers. Messengers play important roles in society. Without them, communication may be hindered. The same is true in the Kingdom of God. Without prophets and prophetic ministry, the communication between God and man may be frustrated.

Messengers are deliverers of the sender's message. A messenger's only task is to carry the message from the sender to the recipient. God calls prophets to deliver the Word (message) of the Lord. Though they may function in other areas in ministry, this is their primary task.

> *But when I speak with thee, I will open thy mouth, and thou shalt say unto them, Thus saith the Lord God; He that heareth, let him hear; and he that forbeareth, let him forbear: for they are a rebellious house. (Ezekiel 3:27)*

Messengers are responsible for the message they carry.
Messengers have to be careful not to lose or damage the
message given them. Some messengers have to deliver oral
messages as well as written. Prophets are responsible for
the Word that God will give them.

> *So thou, O son of man, I have set thee a watchman*
> *unto the house of Israel; therefore thou shalt hear*
> *the word at my mouth, and warn them from me.*
> *(Ezekiel 33:7)*

Prophets are the eyes of the Lord. They have to watch in
the Spirit for what the Lord will say and deliver His
message to the people. If they do not do this, they will not
be successful in ministry and subject themselves to the
discipline of God.

The scriptures call the prophets "watchmen" and
not shepherds. Though God will reveal many things to
them in the Spirit, they must minister those words in
submission to local leadership.

Messengers must not alter the message given.
Messengers have to be careful to deliver the given message
only. The messenger has to be careful not to tamper with
the message in any way. Likewise, prophets have to deliver
the Word as God gives it to them.

> *The prophet that hath a dream, let him tell a dream;*
> *and he that hath my word, let him speak my word*
> *faithfully. What is the chaff to the wheat? saith the*
> *Lord.(Ezekiel 23:28)*

They should not alter the message because of
personal opinion/bias, popularity, or gain. Prophets have to
resist prophesying to earn the favor of men.

In addition, they have to guard themselves against
ministering to bring people under their control. Prophets

that alter the word of the Lord are candidates for becoming false prophets.

Messengers have to be fearless. Messengers have been killed for the message they delivered. Throughout history, there are numerous stories of messengers who are killed for relaying another's message. Therefore, a messenger has to be fearless. Prophets have to be bold in their ministries.

There is no place for fear in the life of a prophet. Prophets must deliver the message that God gives in spite of the consequences. This is why when God called Jeremiah; He encouraged him to be fearless.

> *Be not afraid of their faces: for I am with thee to deliver thee, saith the Lord. (Jeremiah 1:8)*

Numerous prophets have ruined their ministries because they would not prophesy what the Lord said. They would change God's word into one of prosperity, healing, and deliverance without mentioning His discipline, correction, and rebuke.

Messengers have to be trustworthy. A messenger has to have the trust of the one who sends him. The messenger is the link between the sender and recipient. Thus, he has to be trusted in order to have such a responsibility. The Lord entrusts prophets with His Word.

> *Surely the Lord God will do nothing, but he revealeth his secret unto his servants the prophets. (Amos 3:7)*

Prophets are to possess integrity. God chooses to reveal His plans unto the prophets. God will always speak to His prophets as He prepares to move in the earth. Prophets must not take this lightly. They have to be faithful to their ministries.

Prophets as Interpreters

Important to any kingdom are interpreters. Interpreters are there to help foreign nations understand the messages of sending governments and ambassadors. Prophets perform this role in the Kingdom of God.

Interpreters are important to any kingdom. Interpreters are a valuable resource to any kingdom. They provide nations with the opportunity to communicate with one another without confusion. Prophets have always been an important part of the plan of God in the earth. In the Old Testament, God used prophets to reveal His counsel. In the Church, prophets play an important role in the revelation of Christ to the world.

Interpreters understand more than one language. Interpreters have the important task of establishing communication between people of different nationalities and languages. Prophets understand the various manners in which God speaks. They help believers understand the different ways in which God speaks. They are skilled interpreters of dreams, visions, signs, and events.

> *I have also spoken by the prophets, and I have multiplied visions, and used similitudes, by the ministry of the prophets. (Hosea 12:10)*

Prophets have the awesome responsibility to make known unto man the counsel of an invisible God.

Interpreters are skilled in communication. Interpreters are more than translators. It is a known fact that it is possible to lose meaning through literal translation. Therefore, it is imperative that the interpreter be able to not only translate, but also communicate the intent of the words spoken.

Prophets have to be able to communicate the heart and mind of God as well as the Word of God.

Interpreters do not work alone. When an interpreter is present, he is not the primary communicator. The interpreter's function is secondary to those who are conversing, though vital. Prophets do not work alone. Oftentimes, they are seen in groups.

> *And Saul sent messengers to take David: and when they saw the company of the prophets prophesying, and Samuel standing as appointed over them... (I Samuel 19:20a)*

Prophets also work aside other ministries to ensure that the counsel of God is understood. In addition, they labor to ensure its proper application in the Church and in the lives of believers.

Nine Functions of the Prophet

Prophetic ministry is unique. Though there are differences in the administration and demonstration of prophetic gifts, all prophets have essentially the same functions within the Church.

Preach/Teach the Word of God. Contrary to popular belief, prophets not only speak under prophetic inspiration, but also expound on the Word of God. Prophets will preach and teach the Word with clarity. The Old Testament prophets proved to be excellent interpreters of the Law; their New Testament counterpart did the same. They will explain hidden mysteries in the Word.

> *Whereby, when ye read, ye may understand my knowledge in the mystery of Christ); which in other ages was not made known unto the sons of men, as it is now revealed unto his holy apostles and prophets by the Spirit. (Ephesians 3:4-5)*

> *And Judas and Silas, being prophets also themselves, exhorted the brethren with many words, and confirmed them. (Acts 15:32)*

Serve as Intercessors. Prophets serve as powerful intercessors. They have an awesome burden to see the will of God. Prophets will pray for extended times and periods. Scholars call Jeremiah the "weeping prophet." This was due to his continual intercession for Israel.

> *But if they be prophets, and if the word of the Lord be with them, let them now make intercession to the Lord of hosts... (Jeremiah 27:18a)*

Lay Spiritual Foundations. Prophets have the authority and anointing to lay spiritual foundations in the Church. Prophets are equipped to reveal hidden truths of God's Word and lay foundations for the people of God to grow thereby.

> *And are built upon the foundation of the apostles and prophets, Jesus Christ himself being the chief corner stone. (Ephesians 2:20)*

Reveal/Impart Spiritual Gifts (I Timothy 4:14). Prophets have the ability to recognize the gifts of God in believers. They have the ability to impart wisdom, knowledge, and understanding. Prophets can bring to light spiritual gifts resident in believers and impart gifts (by the direction of the Spirit) through the laying on of hands.

> *Now there were in the church that was at Antioch certain prophets and teachers; as Barnabas, and Simeon that was called Niger, and Lucius of Cyrene, and Manaen, which had been brought up with Herod the tetrarch, and Saul. As they ministered to the Lord, and fasted, the Holy Ghost said, Separate me Barnabas and Saul for the work whereunto I have called them. And when they had fasted and prayed, and laid their hands on them, they sent them away. (Acts 13:1-3)*

Prophesy (Acts 11:27-28). Prophets are divinely gifted to prophesy. Their prophecies will be of a greater depth and clarity than other believers who have the gift of prophecy. They will prophesy frequently and accurately. They will have a consistent track record of prophetic words that are true. This is the foundation of their ministry. Though they will intercede, pray, and preach, prophesying is their first priority.

> *Moreover he said unto me, Son of man, all my words that I shall speak unto thee receive in thine heart, and hear with thine ears. And go, get thee to them of the captivity, unto the children of thy people, and speak unto them, and tell them, Thus saith the Lord God; whether they will hear, or whether they will forbear. (Ezekiel 3:10-11)*

Interpret Signs, Wonders, Dreams, and Visions. Prophets are gifted to interpret the supernatural manifestations of God. Some are gifted like Daniel in understanding dreams and visions.

Others will be able to interpret seemingly natural events through which God is speaking. In addition, prophets will see dreams and visions on a regular basis.

> *And he said, Hear now my words: If there be a prophet among you, I the Lord will make myself known unto him in a vision, and will speak unto him in a dream. (Numbers 12:6)*

Expose False Prophets and Doctrines. Prophets are stewards of the mysteries of God. They have revelation and foresight to warn against spiritual deception.

They will contend for purity of faith and doctrine in the Church. They, like prophets of old, will warn and speak against false prophets and ministers, unashamedly.

Jeremiah, the prophet, cried out against the false leaders in his day.

> *The prophets prophesy falsely, and the priests bear rule by their means; and my people love to have it so: and what will ye do in the end thereof? (Jeremiah 5:31)*

Performs Signs, Wonders and Healings. Prophets will have signs and wonders in their ministry. The signs and wonders will manifest to confirm the spoken prophetic word. Isaiah prophesied to Hezekiah that God would heal him. God honored Isaiah's word by granting him a sign.

> *And this shall be a sign unto thee from the Lord, that the Lord will do this thing that he hath spoken; Behold, I will bring again the shadow of the degrees, which is gone down in the sun dial of Ahaz, ten degrees backward. So the sun returned ten degrees, by which degrees it was gone down. (Isaiah 38:7-8)*

Establish Believers, Churches, and Organizations in the Faith and Will of God. Prophets have the chore to bring the people back to the purity of the faith. They have the ability to promote growth and stability in the Body of Christ. In addition, through prophetic insight, they will endeavor to make sure that the plan and will of God is accomplished. Silas, a prophet, accompanied Paul in ministry. As a result, the churches were strengthened in the faith.

> *And Paul chose Silas, and departed, being recommended by the brethren unto the grace of God. And he went through Syria and Cilicia, confirming the churches. (Acts 15:40-41)*

Focus of Prophets

Prophetic individuals operate the same as the brain in the human body. Prophets have the responsibility to communicate the mind and thoughts of God. They will have insight into what God is saying and doing. However, they must be careful not to misinterpret the mind of God based upon their emotions and biases.

Though prophets are keenly aware of the love of God, their words will mobilize people to action after the father-son relationship is established. Prophetic individuals will know how to articulate the Word of the Lord and inspire others to follow His commands. God created man for His glory and for fulfilling His purpose. The prophetic ministry is given to see this fulfilled in the earth.

3
What is Prophecy?

"Thus saith the Lord." This is an expression that some believers cannot wait to hear and an expression that some despise. In spite of these feelings, God has placed this gift in the body of Christ. It is not only reserved for those who are prophets, but for any believer whom the Spirit will use.

It is a widely publicized gift, but many are still confused about its use, function, and purpose. The Greek word for 'to prophesy' is '*propheteuo.*' It means to foretell events and speak under divine inspiration. This means that the source of prophecy is God. No one can prophesy except the Lord gives the revelation.

The Gift of Prophecy

In its simplest form to prophesy means to speak for God under divine inspiration. When someone gives a word of prophecy, it must be a "now" word; meaning, the word should be coming fresh from God. Some things that we call prophecy are really the word of knowledge or the word of wisdom in operation.

Prophecy can be predictive, but this is not its main function. Prophecy is designed to help the believer know what it is the mind and heart of God. Prophecy serves as a testimony of the Lord Jesus Christ being in the midst of His people (Revelation 19:10).

Paul instructed the believers to covet the best gifts, especially prophecy. Prophecy is a direct word from the Lord. It does not come from intuition, feelings, or thought. It comes from the Spirit of the Lord. Whether through a prophet or layman, prophecy always comes with a purpose. In the most basic terms, prophecy comes with edification, exhortation, and comfort.

> *But one who prophesies speaks to men for edification, exhortation, and consolation. One who speaks in a tongue edifies himself; but one who prophesies edifies the church. (I Corinthians 14:3-4 NASV)*

Edify means to erect, build, or construct. When a word of prophecy is spoken, it should help to build up or strengthen believers in their walk with the Lord. Exhort means to encourage or provoke an action.

Many associate exhortation with encouragement only. Though this is true, but there is another side to exhortation. Sometimes, exhortation is given that the people of God may repent and change their ways. The prophetic message may contain elements of rebuke through exhortation.

Comfort means to succor, help, or soothe. Oftentimes, the word of prophecy comes with a demonstration of the love and care of God for His people. This causes believers to be comforted in their trials, tests, and struggles. Whenever a word of prophecy is given, it should accomplish at least one of these three.

The Prophetic Anointing

There are individuals in the Church who are not prophets, but there is a definite prophetic touch on their lives and ministries. These individuals are said to possess a prophetic anointing. How does this differ from someone who has the gift of prophecy? In simple terms, the person who has the gift of prophecy will prophesy on occasion. However, an individual with a prophetic anointing will prophesy frequently as they minister to the Body of Christ.

Possessing a prophetic anointing does not place one in the office of the prophet, but it does make them one of the sons (or daughters) of the prophets. In the scriptures, the sons of the prophets would prophesy, but not with the same level of influence as those called to the prophetic office such as Jeremiah, Elijah, Ezekiel, Joel, and others.

The prophetic anointing is seen oftentimes in believers who are called to the five-fold ministry. They will operate in their respective offices while exercising prophetic insight and authority. The prophetic anointing adds a depth and dimension to their ministries.

In addition, one does not have to be called to a ministry office to possess a prophetic anointing. These individuals are strategically placed in the Body of Christ that all may be partakers of the prophetic ministry.

Individuals who possess a prophetic anointing will prophesy frequently. They will have dreams and visions consistently. In addition, they will be able to recognize and discern the word of the Lord for a particular situation. Their prophecies will be of a greater depth, clarity, and frequency than someone who has the gift of prophecy only.

The Prophetic Office

Every believer is a candidate for this gift. However, what makes the ministry of the prophet different from other believers who prophesy? The answer to this question is simple. The prophecy of the prophet will provide direction, give insight into purpose, rebuke, correct, and reveal future events in God's eternal purpose. This is in addition to edification, exhortation, and comfort. When the prophet ministers, the prophecies will be of greater depth, dimension, and clarity.

The prophet's ministry is foundational. The prophecies of the prophet will often include revelation concerning the will of God for an individual's life and ministry. Also, the prophetic ministry of the prophet will reveal areas of spiritual weakness; including areas of spiritual warfare. The prophet's revelation will be of a greater strength even of those who possess a prophetic anointing, which we will discuss now.

The Spirit of Prophecy

The greatest expression of prophecy is not in the gift of prophecy or in the prophetic anointing. It is in the spirit of prophecy. The scriptures reveal that the spirit of prophecy is the testimony of Jesus.

> *And I fell at his feet to worship him. And he said unto me, See thou do it not: I am thy fellowservant, and of thy brethren that have the testimony of Jesus: worship God: for the testimony of Jesus is the spirit of prophecy. (Revelation 19:10)*

In the Book of Revelation, the testimony of Jesus was the affirmation of Christ's death, burial, resurrection, and supremacy. The spirit of prophecy represents the Church's proclamation to the world of Christ. How does this affect the local assembly?

When the spirit of prophecy is manifested in an assembly, any believer present will able to prophesy even if he/she does not have the gift of prophecy or a prophetic anointing. *The spirit of prophecy comes to unify the Church so that the Church represents one voice* to any unbelievers that are present. Paul alludes to the spirit of prophecy in his letter to the Corinthians.

> *But if all prophesy, and there come in one that believeth not, or one unlearned, he is convinced of all, he is judged of all. (I Corinthians 14:24)*

The only time all believers will be able to prophesy at once is when the spirit of prophecy is present. Paul writes that the unbeliever is judged of all. This means that the unbeliever is faced with the reality of God. This is how the spirit of prophecy is Jesus' testimony. The unbeliever will not be able to deny God's existence through its manifestation.

> *And, thus are the secrets of his heart made manifest; and so falling down on his face he will worship God, and report that God is in you of a truth. (I Corinthians 14:25)*

Now that we have discussed the different aspects of prophecy, we have created a diagram showing the different levels in prophecy. The progression from the gift of prophecy to the spirit of prophecy is comparable to an ocean's geography. The further one goes, the deeper the water. Prophecy manifests itself in a similar manner.

Prophetic Progression Diagram

| The Gift of Prophecy | The Prophetic Anointing | The Prophetic Office | The Spirit of Prophecy |

Greater Depth, Clarity, and Frequency of the Prophetic

The illustration of the ocean is given also to provide the basis for a general warning regarding the prophetic. One must remember to operate in the measure of the prophetic that God gives them.

In the diagram, the further one goes out, the deeper the water becomes. If one operates beyond his measure, he will drown; that is, go into error and kill the prophetic that is within him. Remember, do not try to operate in a prophetic realm for which God has not called you.

4
The Prophetic Vehicle

The word of prophecy comes to believers in different ways. No one way is better than the other. God operates in variety. Therefore, He uses numerous ways to bring His word to us. The manner in which God brings His word to us is referred to as the prophetic vehicle.

vehicle - a medium through which something is expressed, achieved, or displayed; a means of carrying or transporting something.

God uses different means to bring His words to His people for ministry. Paul spoke of the diversity in the operation and function of the gifts in I Corinthians 12.

> *Now there are diversities of gifts, but the same Spirit. And there are differences of administrations, but the same Lord. And there are diversities of operations, but it is the same*

God which worketh all in all. But the
manifestation of the Spirit is given to every man
to profit withal. (I Corinthians 12:4-7)

Just as there are different vehicles in the world, there
are different ways God will impart prophetic
revelation. The most common prophetic vehicles will
be explored.

Voice of the Lord

The widely used prophetic vehicle is the voice of the
Lord. When we state the voice of the Lord, we speak
of God speaking to our spirit through the Holy Ghost.
God commonly brings prophetic words to His people
through direct communication. Once the individual
hears the Lord, they are responsible to deliver the
message that He spoke.

...and he that hath my word, let him speak my
word faithfully. What is the chaff to the wheat?
saith the Lord. (Jeremiah 23:28b)

Contrary to popular belief, God will speak to us most
often in our spirits. The Holy Spirit will speak to us
what God is saying. Jesus said that this is a sign of His
coming.

Howbeit when he, the Spirit of truth, is come, he
will guide you into all truth: for he shall not
speak of himself; but whatsoever he shall hear,

that shall he speak: and he will shew you things to come. (John 16:13)

Some believe that the prophets of Old heard God's audible voice. However, many of the accounts do not state this.

There are times when God's words will come to us through His audible voice speaking to us. In either of these instances, the Word that God speaks can be trusted and ministered with all full authority and assurance.

Dreams and Visions

Other common prophetic vehicles are dreams and visions. These are usually grouped together because each of these communicate God's words through images. There are believers that consistently have dreams and visions.

> *And it shall come to pass in the last days, saith God, I will pour out of my Spirit upon all flesh; and your sons and daughters shall prophesy, and your young men shall see VISIONS, and your old men shall DREAM dreams. (Joel 2:28 Emphasis mine)*

Under the New Covenant, it is common for God to speak to believers in dreams and visions. Scripture shows us that God used dreams and visions to communicate with His people. Visions can be internal (in our spirits) and open (in clear view). We also find in scripture there are certain individuals whom God chose to speak to regularly in dreams and in visions.

> *If there arise among you a prophet, or a DREAMER OF DREAMS, and giveth thee a sign or a wonder... (Deuteronomy 13:1 Emphasis mine)*

At times, the dreams and visions given need interpretation. It is within the interpretation that the word of prophecy is found. In addition, there are times that the dream and/or vision communicates God's prophetic word plainly. In this instance, no interpretation is needed. The dream has to be recalled as it was shown.

> *The prophet that hath a dream, let him tell a dream. (Jeremiah 23:28a)*

Prophetic Perception

Another common prophetic vehicle is that of prophetic perception. In this instance, the word of the Lord does not come to the believer, but the believer perceives and knows what God is saying. Paul alludes to this truth in his writings.

> *Now concerning virgins I have no commandment of the Lord: yet I give my*

judgment, as one that hath obtained mercy of the Lord to be faithful. (I Corinthians 7:25)

Paul gave spiritual instruction to the Corinthians (in this instance) not because God spoke to him directly, but because he knew that what he said echoed the Lord's sentiments. Since the Holy Spirit dwells in the believer, there are times when we will know what the Lord is saying concerning ourselves, others, and occurrences without having any spiritual experience. This phenomenon is the demonstration of what Paul taught when he said we have the mind of Christ.

But he that is spiritual judgeth all things, yet he himself is judged of no man. For who hath known the mind of the Lord, that he may instruct him? But we have the mind of Christ. (I Corinthians 12:15-16)

We can judge all things; that is, perceive what God is saying and doing (prophetically) because the mind of Christ develops in us as we mature and grow in Him.

Prophetic Events

Another prophetic vehicle used by God to reveal His word to us is prophetic events. Common every day events sometimes will reveal the word of the Lord. The prophets oftentimes received what the Lord was saying through natural events. This prophetic vehicle is oftentimes overlooked in the Body of Christ. Yet, if we are prayerful and watchful, God may be trying to communicate with us through events in our lives.

Saul, Israel's first king, disobeyed God continually. He refused to follow the Lord with his whole heart. Through Samuel, God instructed him to kill the whole nation of the Amalekites, including the livestock. However, he spared the king and some of the animals to sacrifice to God.

After Samuel rebuked him for his disobedience, Saul begged for him to return with him. As Samuel walked away from him, this happened...

> *And as Samuel turned about to go away, he laid hold upon the skirt of his mantle, and it rent. And Samuel said unto him, The Lord hath rent the kingdom of Israel from thee this day, and hath given it to a neighbour of thine, that is better than thou. And also the Strength of Israel will not lie nor repent: for he is not a man, that he should repent. (I Samuel 15:27-29)*

When Samuel's garment tore, God revealed to him a prophetic word for Saul. The same is demonstrated in the Church. Seemingly mundane and accidental events are used as vehicles for prophetic revelation.

Prayer

One of the safest prophetic vehicles is that of prayer. Believers are instructed to be consistent in prayer. However, there are believers who receive most of their prophetic revelation during prayer. Prayer is considered a safe prophetic vehicle because attention and focus is placed solely on the Lord.

In the scriptures, Daniel serves as an excellent example of God revealing prophetic information in prayer. He and the three Hebrew boys (men) prayed that Daniel would receive Nebuchadnezzar's dream.

> *Then Daniel went in, and desired of the king that he would give him time, and that he would shew the king the interpretation. Then Daniel went to his house, and made the thing known to Hananiah, Mishael, and Azariah, his companions: That they would desire mercies of the God of heaven concerning this secret; that Daniel and his fellows should not perish with the rest of the wise men of Babylon. (Daniel 2:16-18)*

Daniel prayed that he would receive prophetic information. As he and the others prayed unto the Lord, prophetic understanding and revelation was given to Daniel. If you want to grow in the reception of prophetic revelation, increase your prayer life. You will discover that God is more than willing to reveal things to come.

Angels

Angels are sent by God to aid the believer. Both Testaments agree to the fact that God used angels to reveal prophetic information to his servants. In the Old Testament, we can look to Daniel again. After he prayed and petitioned the Lord, God sent an angel to reveal to him prophetic revelation.

> *And whiles I was speaking, and praying, and confessing my sin and the sin of my people Israel, and presenting my supplication before the Lord my God for the holy mountain of my God; Yea, whiles I was speaking in prayer, even the man Gabriel, whom I had seen in the vision at the beginning, being caused to fly swiftly, touched me about the time of the evening oblation. And he informed me, and talked with me, and said, O Daniel, I am now come forth to give thee skill and understanding. (Daniel 9:20-22)*

God used Gabriel in the New Testament to reveal to Mary of her purpose. While he communicated with her, he revealed prophetic information concerning her cousin.

*And, behold, thy cousin Elisabeth, she hath also
conceived a son in her old age: and this is the
sixth month with her, who was called barren.
(Luke 1:36)*

After the Church was established, God used angels.
While Paul was traveling as a prisoner to Rome, an
angel revealed to him what was going to happen.

*For there stood by me this night the angel of
God, whose I am, and whom I serve, Saying,
Fear not, Paul; thou must be brought before
Caesar: and, lo, God hath given thee all them
that sail with thee. (Acts 27:23-24)*

Some believe this occurrence is rare, but God is the
one who chooses how to deliver His word to His
people for ministry.

The Scriptures

The safest prophetic vehicle is the word of God.
Personal prophetic words that contain scriptures prove
to be rich and powerful. The word of God is a more
sure word of prophecy. It will not change or alter. We
have called it prophecy from the sure prophecy.

*We have also a more sure word of prophecy;
whereunto ye do well that ye take heed, as unto
a light that shineth in a dark place, until the day*

dawn, and the daystar arise in your hearts. (2 Peter 1:19)

God will bring to mind passages of scripture to be quoted to an individual. This type of prophecy will seldom come in error and at the wrong time. If you want a powerful and rich prophetic ministry, study the scriptures.

It will prove to be the basis for a substantial prophetic gift. Though there are numerous ways God can communicate to us, the seven prophetic vehicles mentioned are the most common. There are also many ways to deliver the prophetic word. One only has to follow the leading of the Holy Spirit.

5

The Prophetic Perspective

There is much to consider in the delivery and reception of prophetic ministry. Thus, a proper perspective of prophetic ministry has to be developed. Without a proper prophetic perspective, individuals will begin to despise prophecy because of the errors of others.

> ***Quench not the Spirit. Despise not prophesyings. Prove all things; hold fast that which is good.***
> ***(I Thessalonians 5:19-21)***

When we distrust prophetic ministry, it results in a quenching of the Spirit. God delights in revealing His mind to us through the prophetic Spirit.

> ***But as it is written, Eye hath not seen, nor ear heard, neither have entered into the heart of man, the things which God hath prepared for them that love him. But God hath revealed them unto us by his Spirit: for the Spirit***

searcheth all things, yea, the deep things of God. (I Corinthians 2:9-10)

In addition to despising prophecy, there are others who are afraid to trust prophecy. They fear that they will be misled. To walk in distrust and fear with regard to the prophetic ministry is not the will of God for the believer.

In this chapter, we will discuss how to avoid a major pitfalls in prophetic ministry; namely, in Receiving Prophetic Ministry, Judging Prophetic Ministry, and Applying Prophetic Ministry.

As these areas of concern in the prophetic are considered, the believer should be able to handle prophetic ministry (bad or good) properly.

Guidelines for Receiving Prophecy

To minimize the misery that comes from the mishaps of prophetic ministry, there are guidelines that believers can incorporate in the reception of prophetic ministry.

1) Be prayerful as the prophecy is given. While the individual is giving the prophetic word, pray silently in your spirit for clarity and understanding. This will help in recognizing the source of the prophetic word.

Pray without ceasing. (I Thessalonians 5:17)

2) Listen intently as the word of prophecy comes. Though true prophetic words come with the power and presence of the Spirit of the Lord, try earnestly to listen to the words that are spoken (especially if the prophecy is not being recorded). Sometimes the excitement of receiving a true word overcomes us. This will help in recognizing the intent of the word.

> *Give ye ear, and hear my voice; hearken, and hear my speech. (Isaiah 28:23)*

3) Receive the prophecy in a humble manner. There are times when a person's demeanor or manner will cause us to be hard or stubborn when the word is given. Sometimes, we can miss what the Lord is saying because of this. Even in cases when a prophetic word is impure or bogus, we are to handle them with grace and discretion.

> *Likewise, ye younger, submit yourselves unto the elder. Yea, all of you be subject one to another, and be clothed with humility: for God resisteth the proud, and giveth grace to the humble. (I Peter 5:5)*

4) Consider the individual giving the word of prophecy. There are believers who may give you a bogus prophetic word, unintentionally. Remember to have compassion on the individual. Some will deliver the wrong prophetic word with good intentions. Do not use this time as an excuse to embarrass the individual.

After the time of ministry is over (if possible), talk to the one who gave the erroneous word in private. They may have a valid gift, but moved in error for that moment. If this is not possible, remember to pray for the individual rather than tear down. You have to treat them like you would want to be treated, if you erred in ministry.

> *Brethren, if a man be overtaken in a fault, ye which are spiritual, restore such an one in the spirit of meekness; considering thyself, lest thou also be tempted. (Galatians 6:1)*

5) If the word of prophecy given is true, express this to the one who gave the word whenever possible. True prophetic gifts are under attack. The person prophesying can be strengthened and encouraged to go further in ministry based upon your positive response to their ministry. In this manner, the one prophesying also receives ministry.

> *And we beseech you, brethren, to know them which labour among you, and are over you in the Lord, and admonish you; And to esteem them very highly in love for their work's sake. And be at peace among yourselves. (I Thessalonians 5:12-13)*

If the above guidelines are followed, prophetic ministry (good or bad) can be handled with courtesy and minimize damage in the lives of believers.

Guidelines for Judging Prophecy

One of the major facets of understanding prophecy is to discern when something is not prophecy. Judging prophecy can be a tough task at times. Nevertheless, the scriptures do give guidelines to us to help us as we strive to hear from God through others. We all want to receive from God, but some of us have lost faith in the gift of prophecy.

Many have received erroneous prophecies. Others have followed the directions given to them through prophecy and the results were unfavorable. When judging a prophetic word, we must be careful not to miss God.

Conversely, we need to know when God has not spoken. If you are unsure as to how to hear from God through others, there are certain questions you can ask yourself.

We must understand that God does speak to His people through this gift. We do not need to be afraid, but discerning. Even if we have received bad prophetic words in the past, we should not allow the enemy to steal a blessing from us. God may send someone with a valid prophetic word.

Does it come to pass? Sometimes this aspect of judging is hard to determine. However, if the person prophesying (prophet or laymen) gives a specific period or date for the word of the Lord to happen, it is easier to determine.

When a prophet speaketh in the name of the Lord, if the thing follow not, nor come to pass, that is the thing which the Lord hath not spoken, but the prophet hath spoken it presumptuously: thou shalt not be afraid of him. (Deuteronomy 18:22)

Conversely, do not be quick to brand the prophecy false because it did not occur when you expected it. Prayerfully consider the word. It may turn out to be valid, but you did not understand the time in which it was to happen.

Is it clear and understandable? Though God speaks to us in strange ways at times, the word of the Lord should be understandable; else, you will not know what to do. You cannot obey God if the word is unclear.

For God is not the author of confusion, but of peace, as in all the churches of the saints. (I Corinthians 14:33)

On the other hand, if you do not understand the word, ask the person who delivered the word for clarity. You may find that their choice of words was not clear rather than the prophecy being bogus. There may be times when the person prophesying may not know or remember what was said. However, it is our belief that if the word is from God, they should be able to explain more clearly what they received.

Does it agree with the Word? Prophecy will never instruct you to do something against the written word of God. The scriptures represent the purest expression of prophecy.

> *We have also a more sure word of prophecy; whereunto ye do well that ye take heed, as unto a light that shineth in a dark place, until the day of dawn, and the day star arise in our hearts. Knowing this first that no prophecy of scripture is of any private interpretation. For the prophecy came not in old time by the will of man: but holy men of God spake as they were moved by the Holy Ghost. (2 Peter 1: 19-21)*

Be humble in this area. Not every prophetic word has a direct correlation to the scripture. This is true for prophetic words that may deal with specific situations in your life. Be sure that the word given does not tell you to do anything against the Word.

Is it demonic, fleshly, or the Spirit of God? You must learn to recognize the source of the word. Is it in agreement with the will of God for your life?

> *Beloved, believe not every spirit, but try the spirits whether they are of God... (I John 4:1a)*

Please be wise in this area also. Sometimes, our own personal perceptions may hinder us from receiving from God. If we do not agree with a person's demeanor, we may say it was flesh. Remember, God uses people. Their attributes and personality traits may surface as the Spirit moves through them. Let not your own biases block you from hearing from God.

Does it agree with previous prophetic revelation? Sometimes individuals may prophesy their own will for your life. They will say things that you have never heard concerning you or your life in God. They may try to state prophetically that you are called to a ministry, or that you are supposed to take some sort of new direction in your life. When this happens, judge the word according to previous prophetic utterances from the Lord.

> *This command I entrust to you, Timothy, my son, in accordance with the prophecies previously made concerning you... (I Timothy 1:18a, NASB)*

However, just because someone tells you something that God may not have previously revealed to you does not mean it is not from the Lord. Our walks with the Lord are progressive and so is His revelation concerning our lives.

Sometimes God will reveal something "new" to us in order to guide us into the next phase of our relationship with Him. Be prayerful when new prophetic revelation is given to you. It may very well be the voice of the Lord.

The aforementioned guidelines are to help us in our efforts to receive from God. They are not to be used as excuses to reject the word of the Lord. Sometimes, there will be prophetic words given to which the guidelines may tell you to reject it, but you may discover that the word is from God. Be humble and prayerful while you are trying to judge the prophetic word.

Guidelines for Applying Prophecy

Once a prophetic word is judged to be from the Lord, there are guidelines to applying or handling it. There are many who receive prophecies, but never see their fulfillment due to misappropriating the prophetic word. In order to see the fullness of the word of prophecy, proper application must be done.

1. Rehearse the prophecy in prayer. While in prayer, it is important to discuss the prophecy with the Lord. He may want to give you more information concerning the prophetic word. The scriptures declare that prophecy comes in part. Praying about the prophecy opens you up to further clarification and information.

> *For we know in part, and we prophesy in part.*
> *(I Corinthians 13:9)*

2. Discuss the prophecy with mature believers. Certain believers (leaders and prayer partners) may be able to help you understand other aspects of the prophecy. Sometimes we receive the prophecy in a biased manner. Other eyes may be able to see more clearly what the Lord is referring to with particular prophecies.

> *Where no counsel is, the people fall: but in the*
> *multitude of counselors there is safety.*
> *(Proverbs 11:14)*

3. Fulfill all known requirements for the prophecy's fulfillment. Certain prophecies come with conditions of fulfillment. While you are waiting for God to do His work, do your part. In addition, some prophecies may not specifically outline conditions, but the conditions may be implied. Regardless of the prophecy given, always remain in a strong relationship with the Lord. This will guarantee fulfillment.

> *And it shall come to pass, if thou shalt*
> *hearken diligently unto the voice of the Lord*
> *thy God... (Deuteronomy 28:1)*

4. Walk in faith until you see its fulfillment. The enemy will come to try to strip the believer of faith in the prophetic word. Therefore, fight the deception of the enemy with faith and the words of the prophecy.

> *That ye be not slothful, but followers of them*
> *who through faith and patience inherit the*
> *promises. (Hebrews 6:12)*

Handling and receiving prophetic ministry can be difficult at times. However, if practical guidelines are followed in receiving, judging, and applying prophecy, its operation will be a blessing in your life and not a source of frustration.

BIBLIOGRAPHY

The Bible Library. *The Bible Library CD Rom Disc.* Ellis
Enterprises Incorporated, (c) 1988 – 2000.
4205 McAuley Blvd., Suite 385, Oklahoma
City, OK 73120. All Rights Reserved.

Lockman Foundation. *Comparative Study Bible.*
Zondervan Publishing House. Grand Rapids,
MI, c1984

<u>About Kingdom Builders International</u>

Mission: The primary mission of ATI Ministries is to equip the Body of Christ with tools necessary to defend and contend for the truth of the Christian faith. Jesus Christ came to bear witness of the truth and ATI Ministries is a modern-day extension of His commission (John 18:37). ATI Ministries is a prophetic ministry, distinctively apologetic, committed to defending, equipping, and contending for Christ's Kingdom. Hence, this ministry carries a unique two-fold characteristic, displaying emphasis on prophetic ministry alongside Christian apologetics, in order to effectively communicate biblical truth and inspire a passion for Christ in the hearts of believers.

The primary function of ATI Ministries is to: stand in defense of orthodox Christian faith and practice; that is, for the common salvation and faith that was once delivered to the saints (Jude 1:3), and to equip Christian organizations, churches, leaders, and laity through prophetic insight and biblical instruction (Ephesian 4:12:14).

Vision: Our vision is to see the Body of Christ equipped to proclaim, present, and preach the truth of God, and of Jesus and His Spirit, and of the Holy Scriptures. In addition, to teach leaders and laity how to give an answer for their faith and hope in Jesus Christ (I Peter 3:15). Moreover, to see the members of the Christian faith ready to contend for the faith through sound biblical exposition (Acts 17:2).

<u>About the Author</u>

Roderick L. Evans is a prophetic minister, author, bible lecturer, and Christian apologist. He is the founder of Abundant Truth International Ministries: a prophetic and a Christian apologetic ministry with the commission to defend, equip, and contend for Christ's Kingdom. He is a prolific author, having written numerous books on topics such as Christian orthodoxy, leadership, worship, spiritual gifts, and other areas of Christian thought and practice; as well as, articles, blogs, sheet music, and poetry.

He is the author of two popular blogs, "On D.E.C.K. with Roderick…" and "Moments of Truth," which provide relevant spiritual insights through biblical inspiration.

He travels nationally and internationally proclaiming the message of the Christian faith, equipping the Body of Christ for service, and imparting prophetic revelation through seminars, conferences, revivals, and other sacred services. His desire is to see the Church perfected through the truth of God revealed in Jesus Christ. He and his family reside in Elizabeth City, NC.

Made in the USA
San Bernardino, CA
14 September 2014